Apricots & Thermidor

First published 1978 by Pluto Press Limited
Unit 10 Spencer Court, 7 Chalcot Road, London NW1 8LH

Copyright © Trevor Griffiths

All rights whatsoever in these plays are
strictly reserved and applications for permission
to perform them in whole or in part in the UK must be
made in advance, before rehearsals begin, to
Goodwin Associates, 12 Upper Addison Gardens,
London W14

Pluto Press gratefully acknowledges financial assistance
from the Calouste Gulbenkian Foundation, Lisbon, with the
publication of this series

ISBN 0 86104 206 9

Series editor: Catherine Itzin
Cover designed by Marsha Austin
Printed in Great Britain by Latimer Trend & Company Ltd Plymouth

Two plays by
Trevor Griffiths

Apricots & Thermidor

Pluto Short Plays

A NOTE ON THE AUTHOR

The son of a chemical process-worker who spent much of his life cleaning out acid vats, Trevor Griffiths was born in Manchester in 1935. Unlike his elder brother, he was the right age to benefit from the 1944 Education Act and won a scholarship to a Catholic grammar school. In 1955 he went to Manchester University on a State Scholarship and read English. After two years as a National Service infantryman, he ran a private experimental school in Oldham, taught liberal studies at Stockport Technical College, worked as a Further Education Officer for the BBC, and edited a series of publications for the Workers Northern Publishing Society. He has been a full-time writer since 1972.

His first stage play was *Wages of Thin*, performed by the Stables Theatre, Manchester, in 1969. In 1970 came *Occupations* (about revolutionary politics in Turin in the 1920s), which was also first seen at the Stables and then in the Royal Shakespeare Company's experimental season at The Place in 1971. *Sam, Sam* (two brothers, one of whom stays in his own class while the other moves up and, perhaps, on) was produced at the Open Space in 1972; and at the Edinburgh Festival that year the 7:84 Company performed his two short plays, *Apricots* and *Thermidor*. *The Party*, set in the London flat of a left-wing television producer during the Paris Events of 1968, has been staged twice by the National Theatre: first in 1973 directed by John Dexter at the Old Vic and, later, in David Hare's mobile production. *Comedians* was first produced at Nottingham in February 1975, and later at the Old Vic, September 1975, and Wyndhams, January 1976. *Deeds*, jointly written by Trevor Griffiths and Howard Brenton, with Ken Campbell and David Hare, was produced at Nottingham in March 1978. His work for television includes *All Good Men* (which was also staged recently as a National Theatre lunchtime production), and a 13-part series about a Labour MP, *Bill Brand*.

Apricots and Thermidor*

Apricots is an unusual play, unlike most of Trevor Griffiths' work. Neither overtly political nor about politics as such, it is not a Marxist critique in the sense of *Occupations* or *The Party*. It is, instead, an erotic interlude in a loveless marriage. If anything, it is about sexual politics – but not in the current, colloquial sense.

It was, says Griffiths, written very quickly and 'all of a piece' in 1971. It came directly out of his personal experience (and in that respect differs from his other plays) – a response to his relationship with his wife. He says that he had swallowed whole the myth that women are romanticists and men are realists, that he realised in his own life the reverse was true. That discovery in part prompted the play.

On the surface, *Apricots* is about sex. In the short course of the action the couple copulate and then, in turn, masturbate. On the surface the play is also about sexuality – the characters' self-image as sexual beings. But, says Griffiths, he did not intend the play to be a study of sexuality *per se*, but to use 'perverted', thwarted sexuality as a metaphor for a whole socially-conditioned relationship. Apparently audiences – themselves socially and sexually conditioned to see sex as commodity – found it difficult to look at sexuality as an image of something else. So some found it simply titillating or just embarrassing.

The sex is a symptom of a failed, or at least failing, marriage; a symbol of a barren, non-productive relationship. The couple Sam and Anna – sexual chauvinists both – are sexually inhibited and sexually unhappy. But the source of their frustration is not sex itself; it is their separation and isolation from each other and also from society. Alienated from class struggle, they struggle for power in their personal relationship. Sex is a tool and a weapon. Theirs is a terminal relationship, so they are preoccupied with the past. There is nothing new, so they play old tapes. (The use of the cassette recorder is a concrete, and very effective, symbol of this.) They act out old rituals, repeat past patterns. They are trapped: they don't know what to do, or any way out.

Implicit in the play is the impossibility of considering personal relationships as autonomous – they take their meaning from the conditions of society and the world. Ideological attempts to ignore this are doomed, says Griffiths, just as Sam and Anna are clearly doomed in their marriage. The society reflected in their relationship is futile and introspective – navel-gazing, focussed on 'self', personal well-being and individualistic meaning of life. The play is a metaphor of life in capitalist, bourgeois society.

*Based on an interview with Trevor Griffiths, September 1978

Dream not of gondolas and good wine, but ask how much the gondolier and the wine waiter are getting paid. The characters in *Apricots* are divorced from that kind of consciousness and in that sense lack a relationship with the real world of which sexuality is a part. They are, therefore, essentially divorced from each other – and, presumably on the verge of being veritably divorced.

Trevor Griffiths describes his work generally as committed to analysing marxism and to condemning Stalinism without discrediting socialism in the eyes of the world. But a defence of socialism has to reckon with Stalinism, for Stalinism is the enemy of socialism.

Thermidor is neither an anti-revolutionary, nor an anti-Soviet play, says Griffiths, though it might wilfully be taken to be so by the enemies of the Left. It was an attempt to prise open and examine the frame of mind in Russia in the 1930s when the revolution was still young, but when unsocialist attitudes were beginning to prevail – when people had ceased to matter at all, when the weight of history was pushing hard, when the process of Stalinism had become inevitable. Writing the play was like going inside Ginsberg's 'whirlwind' and discovering an anti-dramatic moment that would illustrate the terrible, inexcusable 'mistakes' that were being made. Hence the quiet, 'human' tone of the interrogation, the concern with old friendships and the welfare of children.

A critical approach to socialism must be historical rather than philosophical, says Griffiths. And sometimes we must necessarily address our comrades rather than a wider audience. This was the case with *Thermidor*, written in 1971, set in 1937 and deliberately intending to parallel the situation in the 1970s, both in the USSR and the UK. If anything Griffiths feels the play is more topical now, with the recent spate of dissidents' trials in the Soviet Union and the hypocritical banner-headline hue and cry about it all in the West. *Thermidor* puts this lingering Stalinism in its historical perspective.

Catherine Itzin

Apricots

Apricots was first performed on June 28 1971 at the Basement Theatre, Greek Street with Peter Sproule as Sam and Tamara Hinchco as Anna, directed by Robert Walker.

Nearly night. The day has been hot; sticky. Now it's cooler, but the air retains a kind of heavy warmth. A garden at the side of a house. Light falls from the house on to the stone strip of patio. There is a kid's swing, an Indian tea-chest painted flat white, a small blocky table, a round-backed chair. On the table, ashtray, cheroots, matches, several bottles of red wine. SAM *lies face down on the stone, as if asleep. A half-full glass of wine stands in the crook of his right hand. A door bangs inside. A baby yowls briefly; is shushed to sleep.* SAM *registers nothing.*

ANNA *in. She is smallish, dark, mid-thirties, fattening gently, still attractive. She looks round tiredly, sees* SAM, *fails to react. Lights a cigarette at the table. Sits on the roundback, legs pushed wearily forward.*

Sam (*finally, not stirring*) All down?
Anna Ahunh.
Sam (*eyes still closed*) That's good.

Silence.

Sam Did you see them?
Anna I saw you.
Sam Big.
Anna All right.
Sam I never saw areolae that brown.
Anna All right.

Pause.

Sam Do you think he minds?
Anna Why don't you get up?
Sam Do you? (*Sitting up.*) Do you think he minds?
Anna I don't know. Tell me.
Sam (*decisive, then unsure*) I'm . . . not sure. He never looked at them once. I watched him. All night he never gave them a glance.
Anna Well. *You* can hardly be said to have . . . neglected her.
Sam He probably does mind.
Anna Mmm.

SAM *stands, drinks, puts glass on table, lights cheroot, fills glass, carries it to the swing, sits carefully down on the narrow strip of wood.*

Sam What's he like?
Anna What?
Sam Pete. What's he like?
Anna What's he like what?
Sam All right.
Anna Oh come on, don't be so . . .

Pause.

Sam You *know* what I mean. Every sodding time we have to go through this boring ritual of rendering down the euphemism. (*Pause; very deliberate.*) Does. He. Fuck. Well?
Anna Yes. Very.
Sam Ah. Good.
Anna Is it?
Sam Yes, I would think so.

Pause. ANNA *fiddles with a bottle, examines a glass.*

Sam I remember you. I remember you when you smelt cleaner than leaves. I remember you when you had clean, firm unpractised breasts. So new. So balanced. And callow daubs of fat on your arse. And your belly was like a dancer's, full of zest, contained. Fucking you then was like running a finger over a green apple. I remember you when your cunt smelt of apricots. (*Pause*) He hated it.
Anna No. He loved it.
Sam Really?
Anna Yes.
Sam Did he tell you?
Anna He loves watching you watching her. He likes your eyes on her breasts. It saves him having you.
Sam Did he say that?
Anna You'll break that swing.

SAM *stops swinging, reaches down for his drink.*

Anna Apricots?
Sam What?
Anna (*spreading legs slightly*) Apricots?
Sam Oh. (*Pause*) Yes.
Anna Come here.

SAM *stays.*

Anna Come here. Come.

SAM *stands slowly, slowly walks over, stands in front of her.*

Anna Now?

SAM *kneels in front of her, pushes his head up her skirt until his lips meet her crotch. He stays for perhaps thirty seconds. Emerges.*

Anna Mmm? (*He doesn't answer.*) What's the word?
Sam I don't know.
Anna I like you best of all on your knees.

SAM *gets up, crosses to the tea chest, sits on it with his back to* ANNA.

Anna Aww. Poor Sam. Poor Sammy. Poor Sammy had his bottom smacked for being a naughty boy. Sammy shouldn't invent nasty lies about Mummy, should he, now! Never mind, soon be better. There, there. There, there, there.
Sam Fuck off, will you!

ANNA *laughs. Lights cut very fast.*
Lights up fast. It's a little darker. Some late redness is creeping in.

SAM *and* ANNA, *still fully dressed, fuck.* ANNA *kneels on all fours, her forearms resting on the tea chest.* SAM *kneels behind her, his lower belly scooping out the arc around her buttocks. The fuck feels real, though there is obviously no genital contact.*

SAM *makes several long, slow, reflective thrusts.* ANNA *stolidly rests.*

Sam Who else?
Anna (*pause*) I should think . . . Margaret.
Sam Yes?
Anna Margaret would.
Sam How?
Anna She'd have you kiss her.
Sam (*quickening*) Yes.
Anna Tongue her.
Sam Yes.
Anna Push your tongue.
Sam Yes.
Anna Inside her.
Sam Yes.
Anna Past the lips.
Sam Yes. Yes.
Anna Past the beard. Past the juice.
Sam Mmmm.
Anna Deep. Deep. Deep.
Sam Tongue in. (*He pushes his tongue out.*)
Anna Would you like that?
Sam Mmmm.

Anna Would you?
Sam Yes.

> *Pause. They gentle down again.*

Sam I don't know that I would.
Anna What?
Sam Margaret. Like it.
Anna Oh?
Sam She's very thin.
Anna So.
Sam And . . . knowing.
Anna Oh? I've always thought she's rather a stupid woman. Ah.
Sam (*quickly*) What?
Anna That's nice. You touched my womb, I think.
Sam I didn't say she was clever. I said she was knowing.
Anna So what does that mean?
Sam Nothing ever happened to Margaret for the first time. That's what I mean.
Anna Mmm.

> *Pause. They fuck on a little.*

Sam You couldn't surprise her with a stoat inside your pants: 'Oh, not stoat again, darling.' Anyway, she's too thin. Are you nearly there?
Anna No.

> *Pause.*

Anna Are you?
Sam No.
Anna My arms are hurting.

> SAM *withdraws, gets up slowly, crosses to the swing, sits down.* ANNA *remains on all fours.*

Anna I didn't say that. I said my arms were hurting.
Sam Same thing.

> ANNA *gets up, smooths herself, picks up a glass, tastes the wine.*

Anna Tea?
Sam Are you making?
Anna Ahunh.
Sam All right.

> *She leaves.* SAM *waits for a moment, then gets up, crosses to the tea chest from behind which he removes a cassette recorder with mic attached. Clicks it off. Kneels, as before. Winds back. Sets it on chest in front of him. Clicks for replay.*

Sam (*tape*) Who else?
Anna (*tape*) I should think . . . Margaret.
Sam (*tape*) Yes.

    SAM's *hand on prick. Begins to masturbate, still on his knees, rocking gently, rhythmically.*

Anna (*tape*) Margaret would.
Sam (*tape*) How?
Anna (*tape*) She'd have you kiss her.
Sam (*tape*) Yes.
Sam Yes.
Anna (*tape*) Tongue her.
Sam (*tape*) Yes.
Sam Yes.
Anna (*tape*) Push your tongue.
Sam (*tape*) Yes.
Sam Yes.
Anna (*tape*) Inside her.
Sam (*tape*) Yes.
Sam Yes.
Anna (*tape*) Past the lips.
Sam (*tape*) Yes. Yes.
Sam Yes. Yes.
Anna (*tape*) Past the beard. Past the juice
Sam (*tape*) Mmmm.
Sam (*on the way*) Mmmm.
Anna (*tape*) Deep. Deep. Deep.
Sam (*tape*) Tongue in.

    SAM *pushes tongue out.*

Anna (*tape*) Would you like that?

    ANNA *returns with tray. She is behind* SAM; *stands and watches in silence.*

Sam (*tape*) Mmmm.
Sam (*closer*) Mmmmmm.
Anna (*tape*) Would you?
Sam (*tape*) Yes.
Sam (*there*) Yeeeeeees.

    He arches backwards, shooting. Holds it for half a minute. Slowly comes to; straightens. Opens eyes. Clicks recorder off. Slowly stands. Turns. Sees ANNA. *They look at each other steadily for a long while.*

Anna (*moving forward, placing tray on table*) That was nice.

Lights out very fast.

Lights up very fast. ANNA *sits at the table, smoking, drinking tea from a mug.* SAM *is standing by the swing. Even darker; cooler too.*

Sam (*emphatically*) Holy.
Anna Rubbish.
Sam Holy.
Anna How? Just tell me how.
Sam I don't know. It just was. Sacramental.
Anna Ah.
Sam Ah what?
Anna Communion? Or confession?
Sam What?
Anna Drink your tea.

Pause. He waits, looking at her.

You said sacramental. I *asked* if you were referring to the sacrament of holy communion or the sacrament of confession.

Pause.

Anna Well?
Sam Neither.
Anna Mmm. Extreme Unction perhaps?
Sam All right.
Anna Well, what did you mean?
Sam (*slowly*) I meant... that once... it used to be... graceful. Full of grace.
Anna Christ.

Silence.

Anna And now it isn't.
Sam That's right. Look, forget it, will you. It isn't that important.
Anna I think you're right.
Sam You would.
Anna What's that supposed to mean?
Sam Nothing.
Anna Drink your tea.

Silence. ANNA *lights another cigarette.* SAM *shivers.*

Sam It's getting cold.

She doesn't answer.

Aren't you cold?

Silence.

Do you want to go in?

Anna You forget . . . natural grace. (*Pause*) Nineteen. I remember dressing that morning. I remember choosing my underwear. Apricot knickers; apple green slip and bra. I remember frothing my pubic hair with talcum powder. I remember dabbing my nipples with cologne. And I remember thinking I wonder what his . . . thing's like. I wonder if it's big, fat, small, thin, light, dark, sallow, hot, cool, red, white. I remember thinking: I wonder what his stuff is like. I've never seen it before. Does it smell? What does it smell like? Is it . . . sticky? Is it hot? Suppose he asks me to . . . kiss him. Take him in my mouth. Suppose he . . . draws himself down the bed and begins to kiss me. Mine. What will I do? What will it be like? (*Pause*) And then I put on my pink pinafore dress and flat shoes and left to meet you at the station. (*Pause*) And later, that night, in York, you said: 'It's never been like this before.' And 'I've never experienced such joy before.' And I lay there and thought: 'But what does it look like?', because you undressed in the dark. 'And what does it taste and feel like?' because you kept it inside your rubber until it was all over, and 'Perhaps he doesn't like cologne and talcum powder,' because not once did your lips move down me. I was, to you, a face and a hole. That's all. I don't think I've ever known such absolute fear in anyone. And now you have the . . . nerve to call it holy.

Long silence.

Sam Sometimes you frighten me.

Silence.

Sam Do you want to go in?
Anna No.
Sam What do you want?
Anna I want you to fuck me.
Sam No.
Anna Yes.
Sam No. I can't.
Anna Yes. You can. You will. I want you to fuck me hard and strong and long. I want you to make my cunt sing with it. Scream with it. I want you to get in there, all of you, I want the whole of you in there, prick and balls and body and mind and senses and conscience and remorse and hope. Everything. I want it *all in there*.
Sam No. I can't.
Anna Yes. You can.
Sam I can't. I can't.
Anna You won't. You mean.

8 · Apricots

Sam I can't.
Anna No. You won't.

> *Long silence.* SAM *walks to the table, picks up his cigars and matches.*

Sam Let's go in.
Anna You go.
Sam Bring the things?
Anna Mmm.
Sam All right. Goodnight.

> (*He bends to kiss her. She doesn't respond. He pecks her cheek. Leaves.*)

> ANNA *sits very still for several moments longer, then puts her right hand between her legs and begins to rub. After a moment she stops takes her hand to her face, smells the fingers. Stands. Lights out.*

END OF PLAY

Thermidor

Thermidor was first performed at the Festival Fringe at Cranston Street, Edinburgh by the 7:84 Theatre Company on 25 August 1971 with Peter Sproule as Yukhov and Tamara Hinchco as Anya, directed by Robert Walker.

Production Note
On page nineteen, the parts of dialogue set in brackets are not to be spoken. They are intended to indicate what the characters would have said had they not been interrupted, but allowed to finish their sentences.

The time is late summer 1937: the place, NKVD Headquarters, Moscow.

A desk, cluttered with papers, files, trays, a phone, blotter, pens, inkwells, intercom, newspapers, a flask, a cup, a tin of biscuits. At it, YUKHOV *reading from a pair of files, his body flicking gently from side to side in his bucket swivel chair. After a moment, not taking eyes from paper, he feels for his cup and takes a small swig of coffee. By the side of the desk, a filing cabinet; a couple of deal tables and chairs line the room walls. A meagre, very cheap carpet on the floor. Somewhere – on the wall, preferably – a large photograph of Stalin and a map of USSR, next to a street map of Moscow with small red and blue markers in it. The phone rings once. He picks it up immediately, says 'yes' followed by 'yes', puts it down, returns to the files. A knock at the door. He calls 'come in,' still reading.* ANYA *enters. She blinks in the brightness of this room, focusses finally on the desk.*

Anya Comrade Yukhov?
Yukhov Come in. Bring that chair and sit down.

She looks for the chair he means, carries it towards the desk, sits on it with a solid show of confidence. YUKHOV *reads on a moment longer, slams files shut, takes them to filing cabinet, replaces them, returns to chair.*

Yukhov (*looking at sheet of paper*) Anya . . . Pakhanova.
Anya That's right.
Yukhov Thirty-seven, Kotka Street, Moscow.
Anya That's right.

He writes something down on the sheet, puts pen down, faces her squarely.

Yukhov You've been called her to answer a few questions. Just a preliminary investigation.
Anya I see. (*Pause*) May I smoke?

She fumbles cigarettes out, offers him one as the exchange proceeds. He declines.

Yukhov If you wish. It would help greatly if you would answer clearly and without frills. My time is paid for by the working people of this country and must be strictly accounted for. Intellectual . . . digressions will not be welcomed.

She offers cigarette.

No.

Anya Very well. I have no wish to waste your time or the people's money.
Yukhov (*taking up pen again*) You were expelled from the party two months ago.
Anya Yes.
Yukhov Would you care to say why?
Anya Don't you know?
Yukhov Just . . . answer the question.
Anya (*pausing, gathering*) I was accused of insufficient vigilance in the matter of Anatoly Kostiuk.
Yukhov To which you replied?
Anya I replied that I had known Kostiuk no better than two dozen other comrades knew him, on the District Committee, and that at no time had I so much as dreamt he was in the pay of imperialist agents.
Yukhov You were found guilty of the charge, nevertheless.
Anya Yes, I was.
Yukhov And given a chance to disarm?
Anya Yes.
Yukhov Which you refused.
Anya Yes. If you wish to put it that way.

Pause. YUKHOV *takes off his glasses; deliberately.*

Yukhov How would you wish to put it?
Anya I find it a far greater crime to my party and to my country to ask its forgiveness for trangressions I *haven't* committed. For in that way, I am asking the party to believe a lie.
Yukhov Would you not agree that, objectively, anyone who refuses to disarm when called upon by the party to do so gravitates towards the position of its enemies?
Anya (*same slight, weary heat*) It depends what you mean by disarm.
Yukhov Not what *I* mean, comrade. Few things could be of smaller significance than what *I* mean by this or that.
Anya Well, what *is meant* by 'disarm.'
Yukhov No, no. No, no, no. (*Lights a cigarette, blows smoke, waves it around with his free hand.*) You do not make a matter *objective* by placing it in the impersonal form. (*Pauses*) You mean, what the party means.

Silence. She looks down, discomfited.

Yukhov Don't you.
Anya Yes, of course.
Yukhov So, objectively, anyone who refuses to disarm when called upon by the party to do so gravitates towards the position of its enemies.

Anya Yes.
Yukhov You agree.
Anya Yes. Except, in my case, I do not believe I . . . gravitated.
Yukhov And tolerance towards anti-party elements leads objectively to disloyalty.

Silence.

Yukhov You agree?
Anya I'm not sure what you mean . . . what the party means by 'tolerance'.

YUKHOV *writes something on a sheet in front of him.*

Yukhov (*finally*) I see. (*Very light.*) How did you come here today?
Anya By bus to Ilinka. Then I walked.
Yukhov When did you last use a government car?
Anya A government car? I don't remember. Round about the time my husband died, I think.
Yukhov When was that?
Anya Last year. April.

YUKHOV *gets up, goes to the filing cabinet, takes out two files from different drawers, looks at them a moment, brings them back to the table, sits down, begins to study them.*

Anya Why?
Yukhov Mm.
Anya Why do you ask? About the cars?

YUKHOV *stares at her impassively, goes back to the files. Finally, finger on a sheet in the middle of one file.*

Yukhov From the record of your interrogation by Comrade Poskrebyshev at Moscow City Party Headquarters. (*Quoting*) Comrade Poskrebyshev: How did you get here? Pakhanova: By car. Comrade Poskrebyshev: Whose car? Pakhanova: A Regional Committee car was sent to fetch me. Comrade Poskrebyshev: Oh? At whose instruction? Pakhanova: I do not know. There has always been a car at our disposal. (*He reads on in silence. Closes the file.*) That was in July of that same year. (*Questioning look.*)
Anya Yes, I'm sorry, I'd forgotten. A car was sent for me on that occasion.
Yukhov But you have no idea by whom.
Anya No, I haven't. I imagined it was sent by Poskrebyshev himself, to make sure I was present for the . . . interrogation.
Yukhov You can't think of anyone else who might have sent it?
Anya No. Of course, we had friends at Black Square. But they were

not people who would dispose of state favours for social reasons. And we weren't people who would ever have wanted them to.

Pause.

Yukhov It must have been nice, having a car at your disposal.
Anya Comrade Yukhov, my husband and I spent ten, twelve hours a day, every day, week in, week out, on party business. We did not use the cars for our own convenience or pleasure.
Yukhov There are many thousands who devote their whole life to the party, Comrade, and never so much as set foot in a government car. (*Pause*) The chit authorizing your use of the car on that particular day was signed by Leped. Did you know him?
Anya Yes, very slightly. We were in the League of Youth together, Moscow Three Division.

YUKHOV *waits*. ANYA *has finished.*

Yukhov Yes?
Anya That's all.
Yukhov I see. That is the extent of your . . . association with 'Comrade' Leped.
Anya Yes. More or less.
Yukhov You weren't ever . . . particularly friendly.
Anya No. No, I don't think so.
Yukhov So it came as, what, a surprise, no surprise, to learn that he was a Trotskyist plotting against state and party?
Anya I can't honestly remember. I don't think I ever really thought about it. He wasn't anybody we'd had any dealings with.
Yukhov Of course. Kostiuk said the same thing. (*Pause*) Leped's confession did, nevertheless, lead to the arrest of some forty-two other fellow-travellers. Kostiuk among them.
Anya But he could not truthfully have named me! I never knew the man, I had absolutely nothing to do with him.

Pause.

Yukhov (*biting*) So you say.

Long silence.

Yukhov (*turning a couple of pages in the file*) You joined the party when?
Anya Nineteen nineteen. February. My twenty-first birthday.
Yukhov Where, here?
Anya Yes.
Yukhov And your parents?
Anya My father was a teacher. Mother was an actress.
Yukhov Ah yes. She was with Meyerhold, isn't that right?

Anya (*wearily*) Yes. For a time. Before his ideas became ... anti-Bolshevik.

Long silence.

Yukhov You worked at the Pedagogical Institute.
Anya Yes.
Yukhov Teaching history.
Anya Yes. Mainly nineteenth century.
Yukhov And now?
Anya (*strong, very straight*) I clean offices.

Pause.

Yukhov (*unmoved*) You edited a university theoretical journal.
Anya Co-edited.
Yukhov Co-edited. (*Turns a page in the file. Studies it.*) With Piatagorsky.

She nods assent. He begins unscrewing the cap on his flask and pouring himself some coffee during this speech. He draws on the file a great deal for what he says, and is often doing little more than quoting chunks of a report filed there. He is in no sense master of the ideas the report handles.

In 1928, an article was published under the title 'Notes of an Economist', written by N. I. Bukharin, who even then had demonstrated for all to see his total contempt for inner-party discipline, besides evincing ineradicable Rightist tendencies. In that article – (*flicking a page in the file*) – he argued that the all-out drive for industrialisation of our country, coupled with a ferocious squeeze on the rich peasant class, was the road to economic, social and political disaster. In spite of the binding decisions to the contrary taken at the 15th Party Congress and in the Plenum of the Central Committee, of which he was, at that time, a member. (*He closes the file, looks straight at her.*)
Anya Yes, I remember the article.
Yukhov Go on.
Anya It was considered an authoritative piece of polemic on the vital question of the rate at which industrialisation should be organised. Four articles stating the Central Committee and Politburo view were published in the same year. (*Pause*) Of course, you realise I was not editor at the time or even a member of the editoral board.
Yukhov But you became one.
Anya Yes. I was honoured to be offered such an important and responsible position on a party journal.

Yukhov If you had been an editor in nineteen twenty-eight, would you have published Bukharin's essay?
Anya (*pausing*) No.
Yukhov Really.
Anya I have always been convinced of the need for rapid industrialisation. I have never considered the matter even debatable.
Yukhov Ahunh. That's interesting. So. It has always been your conviction that rapid industrialisation was of the essence?
Anya Pretty well, yes.
Yukhov You were a delegate to your first Party Congress in 1923.
Anya I was. The Twelfth.
Yukhov How did you vote on the Trotsky opposition programme in that year?
Anya Against.
Yukhov Against?
Anya Against.

YUKHOV *flicks through the file.*

Yukhov (*very deliberately*) It says here . . . you abstained.
Anya (*equally deliberately*) Then it is wrong.

Another pause.

Yukhov Wasn't a part of the Twenty-three opposition programme to do with the rate of industrialisation?
Anya (*uncertainly*) Yes . . . I think it was.
Yukhov They were in favour, were they not, of speeding up the rate of industrialisation? Mmm?
Anya Yes, I believe they were.
Yukhov Then, how come you voted against their programme?
Anya Because I believed then that Lenin's New Economic Policy of gradualism was what the country needed.
Yukhov Go on.
Anya Well. Just that. In nineteen twenty-three our economy simply had to develop, as Lenin himself never tired of saying, on state capitalist lines. Ours was a workers and peasants revolution. If that alliance had been allowed to fail, if we were casually to increase, for example, workers' wages at the expense of the peasant, we should soon have found ourselves facing economic, social and political disaster.

Pause. Plays his trump.

Yukhov Which is roughly what Bukharin was saying, is it not, in nineteen twenty-eight? In your journal?
Anya Yes it was. But by nineteen twenty-eight we had our base. We were ready for our launch, our first five-year plan.

Yukhov (*jotting something down*) You must have heard Trotsky speak many times, in those days.
Anya Yes. (*An attempt at humour.*) We all did. He was hardly noted for his reticence.
Yukhov What?
Anya Yes. I heard him.
Yukhov Did you meet him?
Anya No.
Yukhov What opinion did you form of him?
Anya (*pause*) I thought he was too clever. A dangerous and unreliable man.
Yukhov Did you ever meet any of his cronies? Who were they, Rakovski, Smilga, Radek, Tomsky, you know the people I mean?
Anya No, I never did. (*Pause*) Not Tomsky, by the way. He was part of the right opposition.
Yukhov (*ignoring her*) Now, I find that very interesting. (*Flicking file forward, as though to see how long this particular report is, then returning to the page he's on.*) I have here on file a copy of an article you wrote under the title 'The True Nature of the Bolshevik Party', in which you quote Trotsky quite extensively. How do you explain that?

Long, odd pause. She fiddles for another cigarette.

Anya Don't you know, Comrade Yukhov?
Yukhov What?
Anya I simply wondered whether you might not already know the answer to that question.
Yukhov Confine yourself to the facts. Your . . . reflections are of no importance.
Anya All right. It was an article in *Pravda*, actually. Though it began life as an address to the All-Moscow League of Youth Conference, summer nineteen twenty-five.
Yukhov Go on.

Pause.

Anya The quotation in question is as follows: (*Searching for the words.*) 'Comrades, none of us wishes or is able to be right against his party. The party in the last analysis is *always* right, because the party is the sole historical instrument given to the proletariat for the solution of its basic problems. I know that one cannot be right against the party. It is only possible to be right with the party and through the party, for history has not created other ways for the realisation of what is right.' Trotsky said that, in plenary session, at the Thirteenth Party Congress in nineteen twenty-four. And I copied it down and memorised it. Because I believe it to be true, whether the party now wishes to use me or not, I believe it to be true. (*Pause*) If I remember alright, a Gennadi Yukhov, aged about thirteen, chaired my session and had tea with me afterwards. And talked.

Long silence. YUKHOV *looks down at the file several times, then back at* ANYA.

Anya (*soft, but emotional: a simple statement of her truth*) I never belonged to an opposition, left or right. How could I, when I never had a shadow of a doubt that the party line was correct?
Yukhov (*very low*) Was that you?
Anya Yes.
Yukhov (*looking at her*) Yes, of course.

Silence. Slightly uncomfortable.

Yukhov You've changed.
Anya So have you. You wear long trousers now.
Yukhov Your hair's . . . darker.
Anya Yes. It was summer. It bleaches on top, that's all.

Silence. This mood informs the remainder of the play, though in gradually diminishing measure.

Yukhov (*undermined: tentative: gentled by this embarrassment*) You are . . . you are quoted as saying – (*he reads from the file*) – 'I knew the Trotskyist *Volsky* very well and visited his home often.'
Anya That's not true.
Yukhov You did not know Volsky?
Anya Yes, of course I knew Volsky. We were on the same party committee together. All twenty-eight party members on that committee *knew* him . . .
Yukhov Then what is your objection to the quotation?
Anya I did not say I knew the *Trotskyist* Volsky.
Yukhov But he has been charged and found guilty of Trotskyist conspiracy against the state.
Anya That may be. All I am saying is, I never knew him as a Trotskyist.
Yukhov It will be argued that you displayed a considerable lack of vigilance, Comrade Pakhanova.
Anya And I will argue that it's a lack I share with the whole of that district committee.
Yukhov Comrade Pakhanova, I think I should warn you that you would be advised to forget that line of defence tomorrow. It is sufficient – –
Anya Tomorrow? You mean I am to come back *tomorrow*? There was nothing on the card about tomorrow.

Yukhov Comrade, you should realise, things are very serious for you here.
Anya I don't believe I can manage tomorrow. I have my family to take care of.
Yukhov I'm afraid there is little to be done about that, Comrade. There is very little to be done about anything, once charges have been laid and . . . (due legal processes set in motion).
Anya (*with sharpening alarm, merging into mild hysteria*) Charges? What charges?
Yukhov Comrade Pakhanova . . . (I have been trying to tell you . . .).
Anya What charges? I know nothing about charges.
Yukhov I'm trying to tell you, Comrade . . .
Anya You said nothing about charges. There was nothing . . . (on the card about charges . . .).
Yukhov (*fist*) Will you *listen* to me!

> *She is dead silent; trembles a little. He is embarrassed again, worried by the silence and her terror. Gently, but wanting the business ended.*

> Comrade, I have here a warrant for your arrest. It was issued last week, over the signature of Comrade Yezhov. The charges include 'political shortsightedness', 'lack of vigilance' and 'compromised with dubious elements'. (*Pause*) A more detailed specification of the charges will be drawn up as a result of this interview. Please read it. (*Pause*) Please read it!

> *She cannot bring herself to read it, shakes her head from side to side. Subsides.*

Anya (*small; dead*) What will happen to my children?
Yukhov I don't know.
Anya What will happen to my children? I have three small children. What will happen to them?
Yukhov I'm sorry. You mustn't ask me. My brief does not extend to the welfare of your children.

> *Pause.*

Anya Will I be allowed to see them?
Yukhov That may well depend upon whether you are willing to sign . . . a form of confession.
Anya I have nothing to confess.

> *Pause.*

Yukhov You knew the Trotskyist Volsky socially.
Anya (*dull; weary, rather hopeless*) I knew *Volsky* socially.

Handwritten margin note: "The limits of political/personal"

Yukhov But since Volsky is a convicted Trotskyist traitor, objectively, therefore, you knew the Trotskyist Volsky.

Anya Comrade Yukhov, please don't play these silly games with me. You will only waste your time and the people's money.

Yukhov (*doggedly*) Please answer. I asked you whether you agree that, objectively, you knew the Trotskyist Volsky.

Anya (*starting low, but building, some small fight left there*) There is no power in the world that can give you the right *to tell me what I know*. The I is *me*, comrade. Me. *I know* means all those things I have seen and smelt and tasted and touched and held, all those people I've talked to and waited for, married, slept with, given birth to; all those ideals I have fought for and believed in. (*Pause. Strong now.*) And *I* am the *only* subject of *know*. You cannot *tell* me I knew the Trotskyist Volsky. I knew Volsky the father of two teenage daughters. I knew committeeman Volsky. I knew Volsky the husband of fat-faced Katya with the red hair and bad teeth. *That* Volsky I knew. No other. No other.

Long pause.

Yukhov (*jotting a note*) No matter. In time you will come to realise that for most purposes there is very little difference between 'subjective' and 'objective'. Tomorrow you will meet Principal Investigator Baumann. If I could offer you one word of advice, try to drop your superior intellectual tone with him. He is, if it is possible, even less interested in . . . philosophical speculation . . . than I am.

Anya (*very low, broken, reflective*) What has happened to you? You used not to be so . . . inert. I can remember you, you know, that July day. You were so alive. You wanted to know everything. You asked me so many questions over tea I could hardly keep pace with you . . . (And) you told me about your father, how he had scrimped and saved to buy you books for your studies. And how ambitious you were then! To serve . . . the revolution. What has happened? What has happened to us?

Yukhov (*Intercom. It's impossible, but he tries to say it so that she does not hear him.*) Warder please. Cellars, yes. (*To her.*) That's all for the moment. (*Tidying files.*) There'll be more tomorrow. Colonel Baumann is a busy man, as you can imagine. Some sort of confession would have been a great help, but . . . Through that door. There'll be someone waiting.

Anya This is a *soviet institution*. You cannot treat people this way in a soviet institution.

Yukhov Enemies . . . are no longer people.

Anya (*standing, moving, turning*) What about my children? I have three small children.

the banality of evil

Yukhov They will be attended to. (*Pause*) Our children are our future.
Anya I'm innocent. You know that, don't you. I'm innocent.
Yukhov Are you?

She leaves. He stretches. Drains his mug. Returns files to cabinet.

Poskrebyshev now. Then lunch.

END OF PLAY

Also available from Pluto Press

Caryl Churchill	Light Shining in Buckinghamshire	£1.50 pbk
Caryl Churchill	Traps	£1.50 pbk
Margaretta D'Arcy and John Arden	The Non-Stop Connolly Show Parts 1 and 2	£1.50 pbk
Margaretta D'Arcy and John Arden	The Non-Stop Connolly Show Part 3	£2.00 pbk
Margaretta D'Arcy and John Arden	The Non-Stop Connolly Show Part 4	£2.00 pbk
Margaretta D'Arcy and John Arden	The Non-Stop Connolly Show Part 5	£2.00 pbk
Margaretta D'Arcy and John Arden	The Non-Stop Connolly Show Part 6	£2.00 pbk
Steve Gooch	Female Transport	£1.50 pbk
Steve Gooch and Paul Thompson	The Motor Show	£1.50 pbk
Steve Gooch	Will Wat? If Not, What Will?	£1.50 pbk
Steve Gooch	The Women Pirates: Ann Bonney and Mary Read	£1.50 pbk
Trevor Griffiths	The Cherry Orchard (Anton Chekhov)	£1.50 pbk
John McGrath	The Cheviot, The Stag & The Black Black Oil	£1.00 pbk
John McGrath	Fish in the Sea	£1.50 pbk
John McGrath	The Game's A Bogey	£0.90 pbk
John McGrath	Little Red Hen	£1.50 pbk
John McGrath	Yobbo Nowt	£1.50 pbk
Paul Thompson	The Lorenzaccio Story	£1.50 pbk

Plus

Franz Xaver Kroetz	Farmyard and Four Plays	£2.70 pbk
		£6.60 hbk

Pluto Plays 1978–79

Pluto Plays

Margaretta D'Arcy and John Arden The Little Gray Home in the West*	£2.45 pbk
Nikolai Erdmann The Suicide Man*	£1.95 pbk
Dario Fo We Can't Pay? We Won't Pay!	£1.95 pbk
Wilson John Haire The Bloom of the Diamond Stone*	£1.95 pbk
Red Ladder Taking Our Time*	£1.95 pbk
David Rudkin Sons of Light*	£2.45 pbk
Snoo Wilson The Glad Hand*	£1.95 pbk

Pluto Short Plays

CAST Confessions of a Socialist*	£1.25 pbk
David Edgar Ball Boys	£1.25 pbk
Dario Fo The Boss's Funeral*	£1.25 pbk
Trevor Griffiths Apricots and Thermidor	£1.00 pbk
Sam Shepard Suicide in B Flat	£1.25 pbk
Snoo Wilson A Greenish Man*	£1.25 pbk

These plays are also available on subscription at advantageous rates (at least one-third off the published price) for each series (of 12 plays per year) separately or both series (twenty-four plays per year) together. Further information and subscription forms available from: Pluto Press, Unit 10 Spencer Court, 7 Chalcot Road, London NW1 8LH (01–722 0141).

* Not yet published

PR
6057
.R52
A83